This book is dedicated
to future singers and song writers.
May they
find creative words to
sing through
life and inspire others.

Fifty percent of all proceeds from the sale of
this book will be donated to
Special Olympics.

ISBN 978-0692369111
Text copyright © 2015 by Kristy Ann Moore
Illustrations copyright © 2015 by Kristy Ann Moore
Printed in the U.S.A.

Song Ideas

Write a song about:

A

an actor	an acrobat	an airplane
an alligator	an apple	an armadillo

B

a baby	bacon	a balloon
barbecue	the beach	a bumblebee

C

a camel	camping	a cat
a chicken	a computer	a city

D

a diver	a doctor	dodgeball
a dog	a dolphin	a donut

E

an egg	an elephant	an eraser
an escape	exercise	an eyeball

F

a feast	a fiasco	a fiesta

More Song Ideas

G

a gem

a genie

a ghost

a giant

the giggles

a gray goat

H

a headache

a helicopter

hockey

hiking

a horse

a house

I

ice

an idea

an igloo

ink

an island

ivy

J

a job

a joke

a journey

a judge

a jungle

a jury

K

a kangaroo

a key

a kitchen

a kite

a kitten

knowledge

L

a ladybug

a lamp

laughing

a leaf

a lemon

love

More Song Ideas

M

magic   a map   a medal

a memory   mice   a monkey

N

a necklace   a neighborhood   nightfall

a notebook   a nurse   a nursery rhyme

O

the ocean   an outlaw   an oval

an owl   an ox   an oyster

P

paint   pajamas   a park

peace   a pebble   a pet

Q

a quarter   a quarterback   a queen

a question   a quilt   a quiz

R

a rabbit   a race   rain

a rhyme   a river   a road

More Song Ideas

S

| a sandwich | a safari | school |
| a seahorse | a shark | shopping |

T

| talking | a teacher | a test |
| thinking | thunder | a toad |

U

| an umbrella | an umpire | underground |
| a unicorn | unity | upholstery |

V

| a vacation | a van | a vase |
| victory | a violin | a vowel |

W

| a wagon | a weasel | the weather |
| a wildcat | the wind | winter |

X   x-ray   xylophone   **Y**   a yak   yo-yo

Z   zebra   zero   zigzag   zipper   zoo

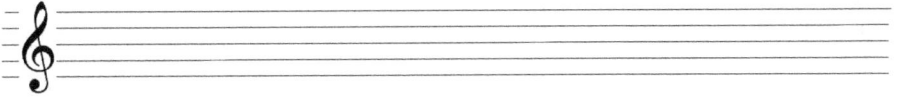

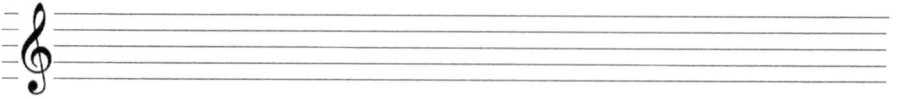

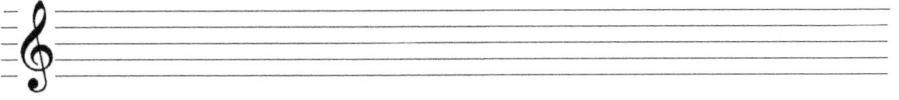

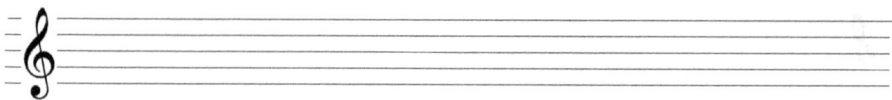

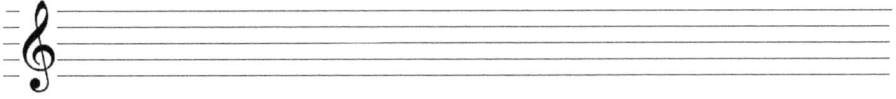

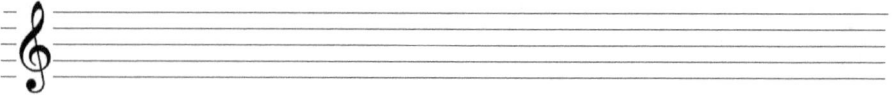

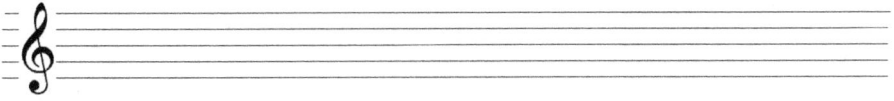

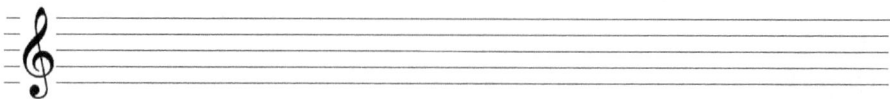

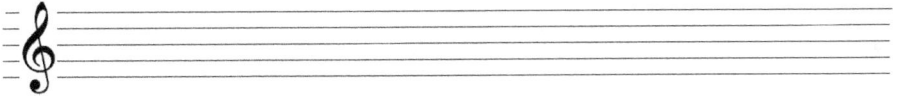

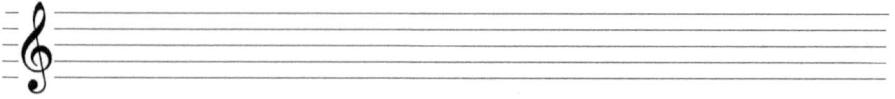

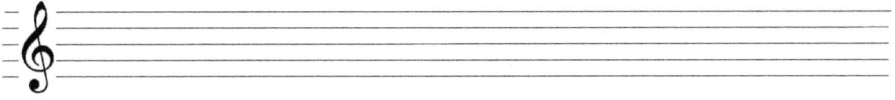

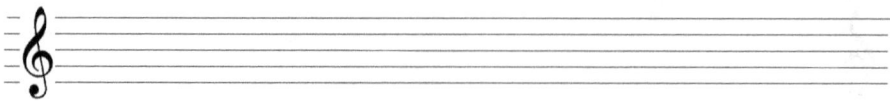

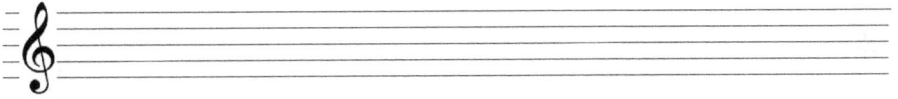

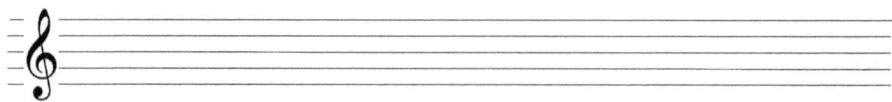

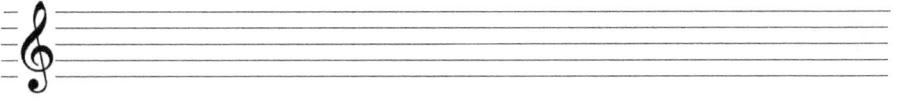

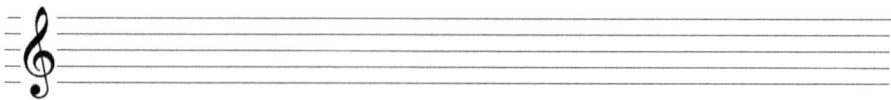

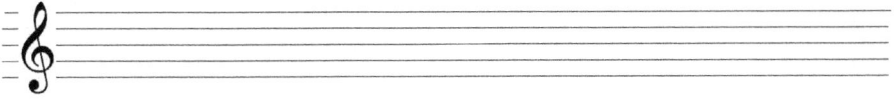

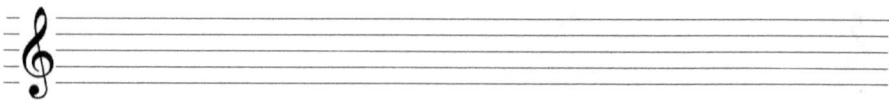

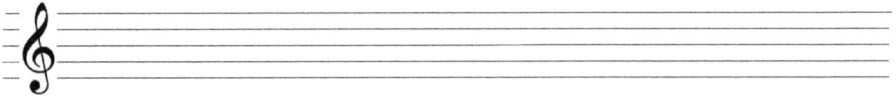

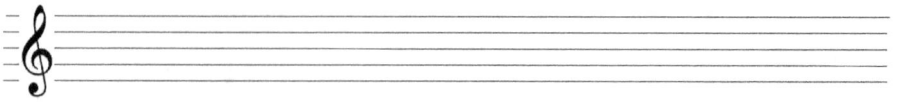

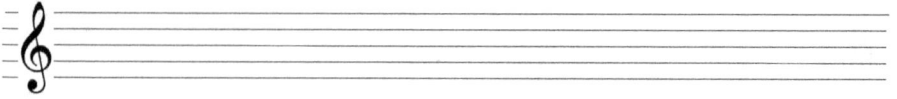

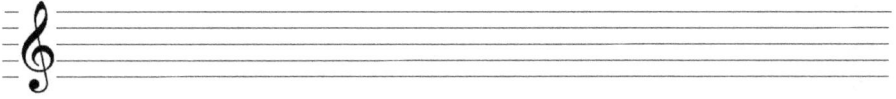

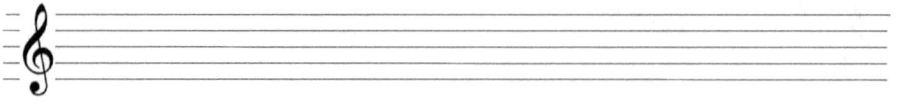

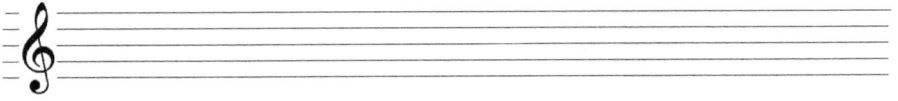

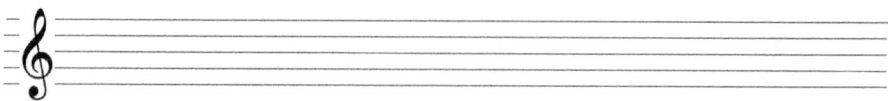

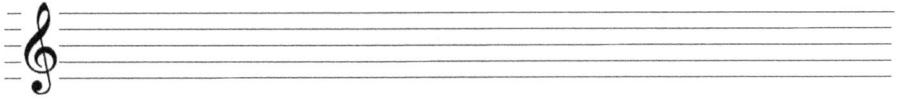

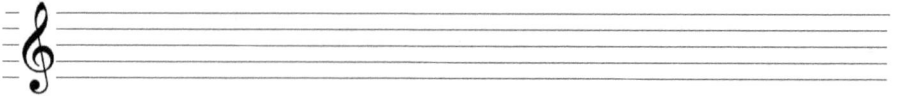

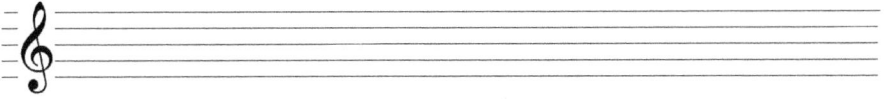

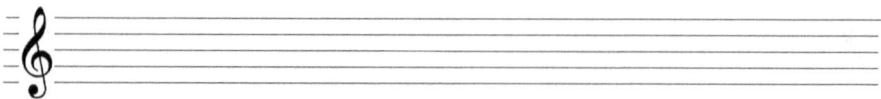

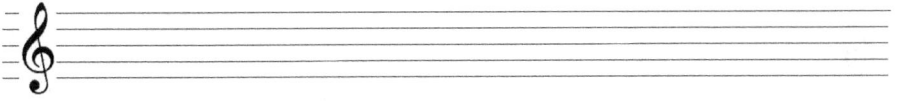

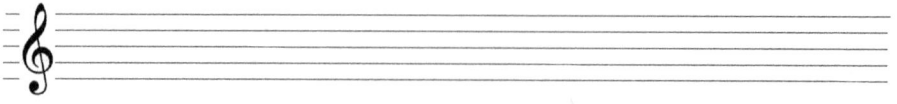

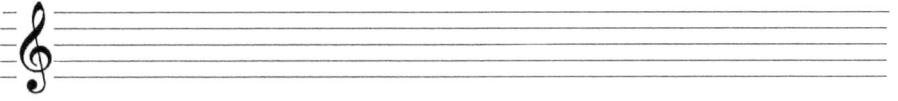

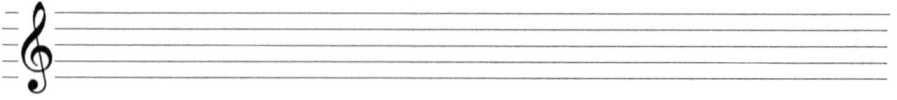

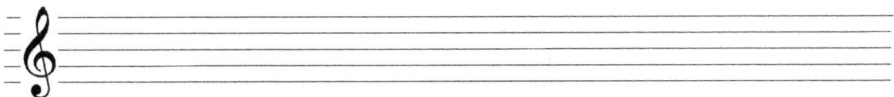

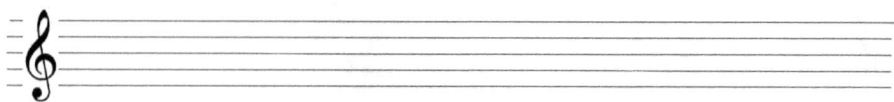

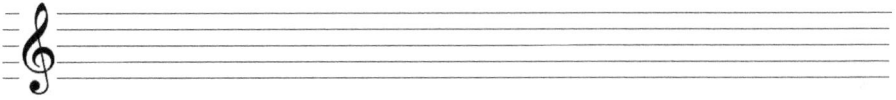

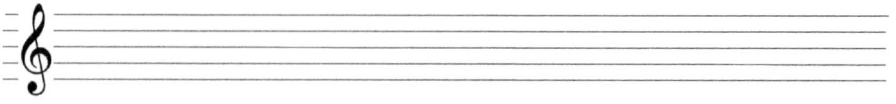

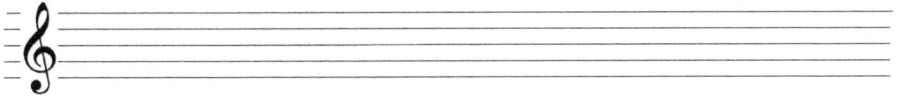

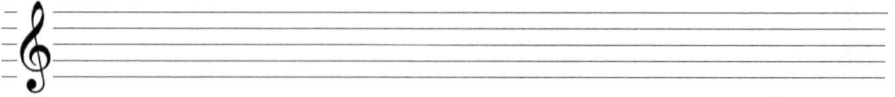

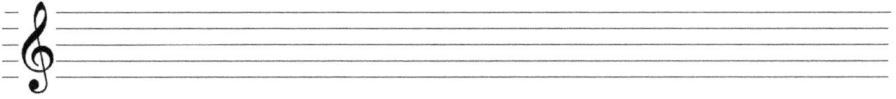

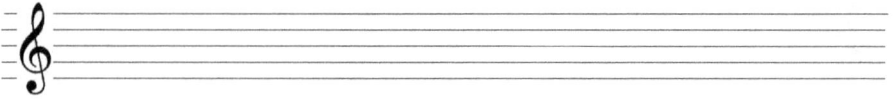

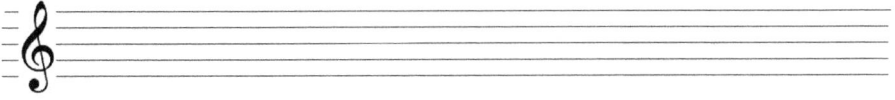

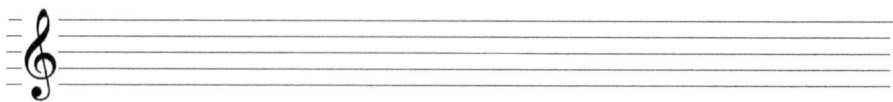

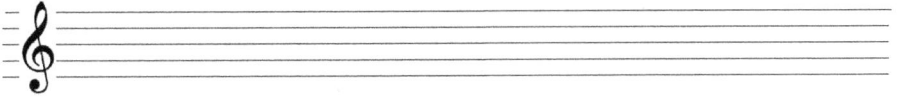

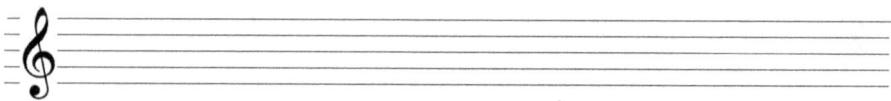

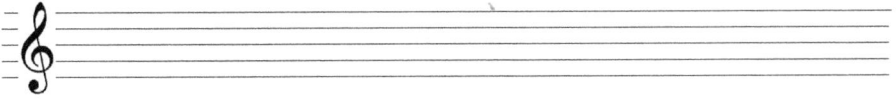

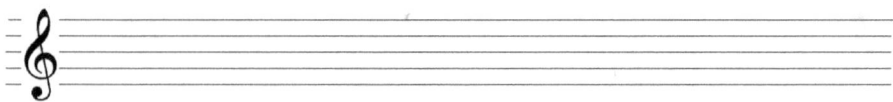

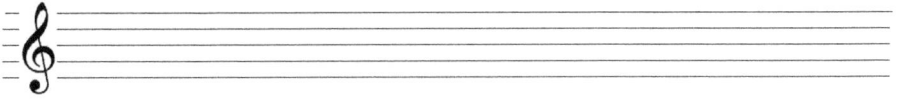

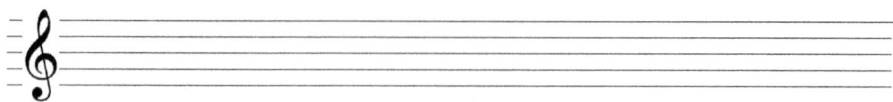

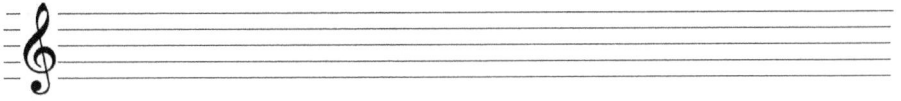

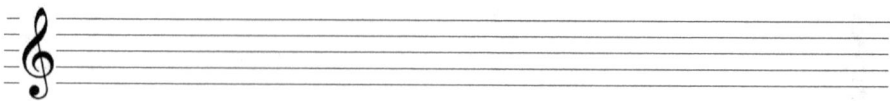

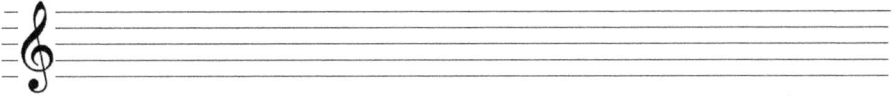

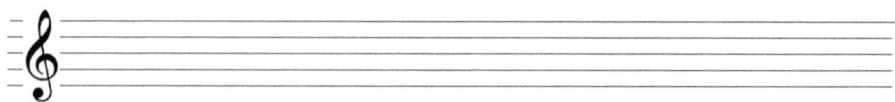